AF271058

CHICAGO
from the AIR

WHITE STAR
PUBLISHERS

CHICAGO

from the AIR

CONTENTS

Text
Marcella Colombo
Gianfranco Peroncini

Photographs
Antonio Attini

Graphic design
Maria Cucchi

Translation
C.T.M., Milan

© 2002 White Star S.r.l.
Via C. Sassone, 22/24
13100 Vercelli, Italy
www.whitestar.it

All rights reserved. No part of this publication may
be reproduced, stored in a retrieval system or
transmitted in any form or by any means,
electronic, mechanical, photocopying, recording
or otherwise, without written permission from
the publisher.

ISBN 88-8095-754-6
2 3 4 5 6   06 05 04 03

Printed in Korea by Samhwa Printing Co.
Color separation: Chiaroscuro - Turin

1 With its clock tower, the Wrigley Building is one
of the most distinctive constructions in Chicago.

2-3 This is the Chicago lake front with the Navy
Pier in the foreground to the north of the Chicago
River. It is home to more than 998 acres of parks,
gardens, boutiques, restaurants, fountains, food
kiosks, a giant panoramic wheel, and a fleet of boats
offering relaxing cruises on the lake.

4-5 In the center of Chicago, the pointed dolmens
of the first civilization and city to build towards
the sky typify the American preoccupation with
growth and expansion.

6-7 Chicago in the rain: imposing shadows chase
one another from the banks of majestic Lake
Michigan through the busy streets of the city center.

8 and 9 The silhouettes of the skyscrapers along
Michigan Avenue are the result of a layout that has
produced unique views.

10-11 The aerials on the roof of the John Hancock
Center overlook the shores of Lake Michigan in the
heart of downtown.

12-13 Skyscrapers, traffic, lights, and business: the
panorama of a downtown that keeps pace with the
most active and feverish of third millennium cities.

INTRODUCTION

Chicago is not just the Loop and the Magnificent Mile. Neither is it the account, the face, the colors, lines, drawings and materials of the most daring innovations in international architecture, nor is it Lake Michigan, the series of city parks, the beaches, the melting pot of a thousand cultures, flavors, smells, memories, anxieties and dreams of the many peoples that have made the United States what it is (there are more Poles in Chicago than in any city in Poland except for Warsaw). It is not just these things, it is all of them. The plot of a story that seems like a novel is woven among the thousand records of this inimitable city, against the background of these skyscrapers, on the waves of Lake Michigan and above and beneath the bridges of the Chicago River. Following the Great Fire in Chicago, whilst its ashes were still hot, the plan was drawn up that was to bring the Big Onion into existence, the metropolis that formed the meeting point of the north and south, and east and west of the United States of America. Chicago lies at the heart of the Midwest and is the most American and futuristic city in the USA. As Oscar Wilde wrote, the youth of America is its oldest tradition.

Chicago is the land of paradoxes: green parks and skyscrapers, the lake, sailing boats, jogging and a business district where, minute by minute, wealth is created and destroyed. It is the intersection of the horizontal lines of the Great Plains with the vertical ones of the lay cathedrals that pierce the sky. The writer Nelson Algren captured the spirit of this kingdom of the oxymoron when he described it as a beautiful woman with a broken nose. Slaughterhouses and Impressionist art galleries exist side by side.

14

14 bottom left The white dome of the Baha'i House of Worship (187 feet high) in the Wilmette district in Chicago's northern suburbs. The design was produced in 1909 but construction only began in 1920 and was completed in 1953.

14 top right These are the skyscrapers that dominate the Gold Coast district, an area of land reclaimed from Lake Michigan using the rubble from the Great Fire of 1871.

15 The very center of Chicago's financial district. The 33 feet tall aluminium statue of Ceres, the Roman goddess of grain and agriculture, dominates the 45 story Art Deco building of the Chicago Board of Trade.

16

Smart businessmen, the cops and robbers of the Roaring Twenties, blues, jazz, the roar of machine guns, Al Capone and Louis Armstrong, the Biograph cinema where John Dillinger – Public Enemy No. 1 (one of the many) – ended his days. Chicago, Chicago, 'that toddling town...'

The skyline is unmistakable and the lake is so large it looks like a sea. The city is a jumble of emotions, lights, and sounds. It is a river in flood that welcomes the gawping visitor to the heart of the Loop, the center that, block after block, building after building, sums up, overlays, repeats and discriminates the most superb architecture ever to have been spawned by the human genius. At the start of the 1900s it was known as the "city near hell" because of the open air skeleton it unashamedly displayed, like the surface railway that spoilt the roads, yet which today seems attractive and inspired.

Chicago rose again after the Great Fire of 1871 but in previous decades it had been redeemed from the mud and marshes created where the Chicago River met Lake Michigan. In just three years, from 1855 to 1858, the levels of all the streets were raised and the houses removed from the quagmire and given new foundations. This was how Chicago prepared itself for the construction of its surprising architecture and succeeding in turning the disaster of the devoring fire into an opportunity for progress. New projects, new buildings and new horizons. The rubble from the destroyed buildings provided filling material for areas reclaimed from the lake. From that moment, the ascent towards the sky began and the city's destiny was written in reinforced concrete, steel, marble, granite and glass by such masters as Frank Lloyd Wright, Ludwig Mies van der Rohe, and Helmut Jahn. The rest is history.

16 The region of Chicago in a photograph taken from the Shuttle appears as a huge, third millennium conurbation of eight million inhabitants.

16-17 Great
Chicago faces onto
the southern bend
of Lake Michigan
where it is met
by the Chicago
River. This river has
been a determining

factor in the success
of the city by
putting it in
communication with
the Great North
and, via a system of
canals, with the
Atlantic Ocean.

18-19 The dance of
giants in the center
of Chicago celebrates
the conquest of
vertical space which
began here and
marked a decisive
step in international
city planning.

20-21 Chicago is
not just a business
and hi-tech city. It
is also a pearl set in
the natural setting
of stunning Lake
Michigan.

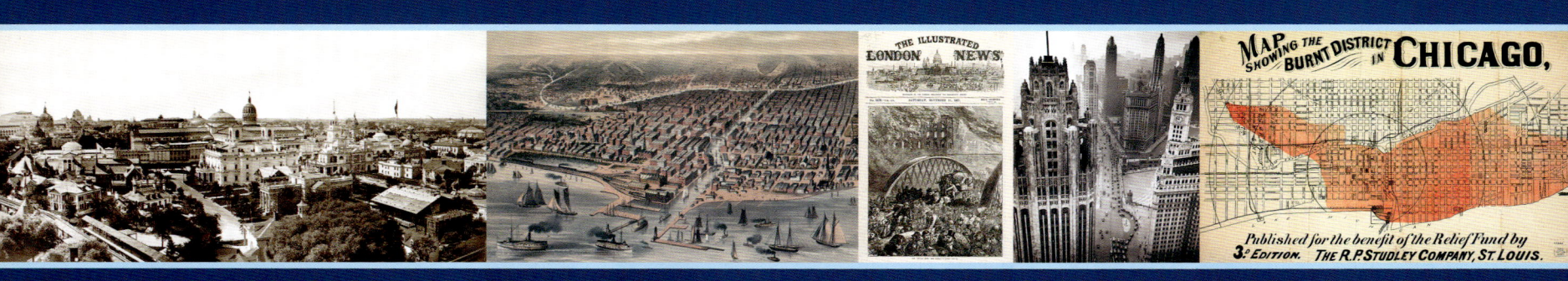

 # HISTORY

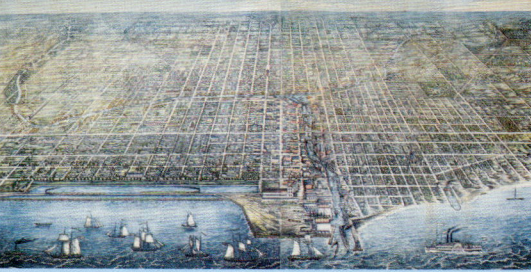

CHICAGO IN 1820.

The First SETTLER of Chicago in the year 1820

24 top This lithograph, by J. Gemmel from the 1850s, shows Chicago in 1820. Lake Michigan had no natural port or shelter and it was only after engineering work in 1835 that the first ship of a hundred tons or more was able to sail up the Chicago River.

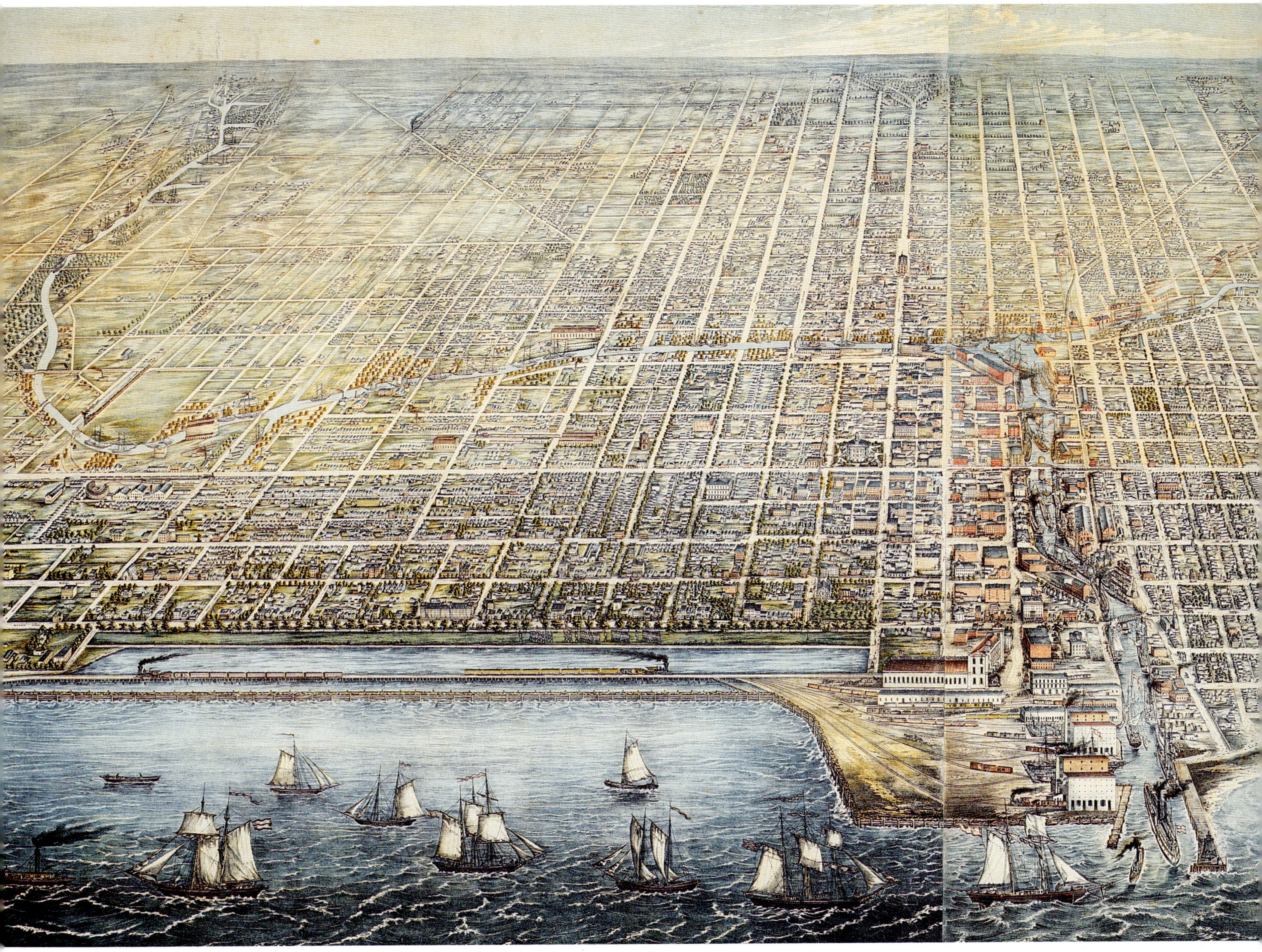

T he skyline soars up vertically to look for the clouds in the sky, as the sun's rays climb the walls of the skyscrapers that have symbolized the history of Chicago and the USA. The horizon is sketched out by the strength of steel, covered in marble, stone, and glass. Urban ravines, gorges, and canyons carved into streets, avenues, and

boulevards have been created by the scalpel of convex erosion, overturned, ever contrary to the natural laws that hollow out into the deep. A longing for infinity, an arrogant architectural pride reaches out and dominates the environment. On the threshold of the Great Plains, that stretch out towards the immense spaces of the Pacific, the territories, prairies, and mountains still feel the effects of the argumentative anxieties of the Old World.

Chicago is the town of records and excesses, prohibition and the Untouchables. But it is also the town of Walt Disney and Hemingway, *Playboy* and the McDonald's chain, Al Capone, Louis Armstrong, and Michael Jordan. It's the capital of American architecture, and for some, it's the most beautiful city in the world. It rose up on the shores of Lake Michigan, a body of water nearly four times bigger than Jamaica, and was literally reborn from its ashes like the Phoenix after a catastrophic fire. Chicago is The Big Onion, named after the Native American *checagou*, an exotic, fascinating word that denotes the *Allium cepa*, a humble but tasty onion that flourished in these parts. It is an entirely different thing from The Big Apple, New York, with other colors, other flavors, and a different history. Chicago has always reached out for and tried to go beyond the limit. It boasts the

busiest airport in the world, the first skyscraper, the biggest inland port, the biggest cereals market, the biggest private building, the largest number of Nobel Prize winners, and arguably the highest skyscraper in the world (it is just a question of an aerial, they say here). The list could go on to include sights such as the Congress Center, the Aquarium, the Chicago Public Library, and the rail terminal, not to mention hot dogs and even, if you believe it, the tastiest pizza.

It is not by chance that the cultural and architectural schools and courses that trace out American space in the two main directions, the vertical and horizontal, have flourished in Chicago. The magic of the needles that puncture the sky, such as the famous Sears Tower, Oak Park, the Chicago School and the Prairie School, and Frank Lloyd Wright can or could be found here: these are the keys by which Chicago entered into the heart of twentieth century architectural development. The Chicago School was born under the sign of skyscrapers, the first on the contemporary urban horizon. The center of the city is a concentration of the architectural styles that defined the history of US and international architecture within the space of a few decades. To walk around this area with your eyes wide open is like leafing through a book on urban architecture, taking

24-25 This detail of an 1857 lithograph gives an aerial view of Chicago. The shore of the lake is dotted with warehouses and piers at the mouth of the Chicago River where wood and grain was stored and loaded.

25 top This is where the North and South Branches of the Chicago River meet, in an aquatint by Raoul Varin. The scene is set in 1833 and shows the first settlements observed suspiciously by the local Indians.

part in an open air lesson in style, history, and aesthetics. Buildings have become icons; historic monuments which, in The Loop, the most vital and dynamic business quarter of the city, take on their main and most evident role of 'machines for living,' built to accomodate thousands. Quite the opposite of the Prairie School, the architectural design creature of Frank Lloyd Wright whose most authentic dimension can perhaps be measured by the pace and rhythm of houses developed for individuals. And it was in the lush green residential quarter of Oak Park that Wright took the first and most significant steps in his professional adventure, with the setting up of his workshop of ideas between 1899 and 1909 in his house and studio where, with the assistance of 15 students, he created 150 designs and defined the fundamental principles of his school.

This is one of the splendid

26 top The print shows the Great Fire of 1871 that completely destroyed the city. The fire began on the night of October 8 and may have been started by an oil lamp that fell over in the barn of the O'Leary family.

26 bottom A 1871 New York print shows the dramatic destruction of Chicago. The fire razed 100,000 houses to the ground and burned almost 300 people to death.

oxymorons of Chicago, the juxtaposition of contrasts in the resolution of opposites. It is almost in a Zen dimension, and this is certainly one of the elements that best identifies the city and makes it unique and extraordinary. From the search for an ultramodern Gothic, a kind of deconsecrated reaching towards the sky, to the struggle between the environment and nature, where the straight, endless horizon of the Great Plains in the west underlines the integration of inner and outer spaces, Chicago is a place where the walls stop being walls and become mobile screens.

It all started when the terrible fire on October 8, 1871 razed the first Chicago to the ground like a modern Troy, left defeated and smoking. This had been the Chicago founded in 1779 by Jean-Baptiste Point du Sable, the courageous son of the Quebec fur trader and a black slave. Starting from a mud hut at the mouth of the Chicago River, he consolidated a trading post that worked alongside with Native Americans, the English, and the French, an explosive threesome among whom there was little love lost at that time. As the natives later said, the first white man to arrive in these parts was a French-speaking black man.

Growth was slow. Illustrious figures from that period of exploration passed through *Checagou*

26-27 This is how the city appeared in the days before the Great Fire. A modern claim for the cause of the fire is a shower of meteorites which devastated nearly 1,000,000 acres of forest around Pestigo in Wisconsin on the same night.

27 bottom The areas affected by the Great Fire. The O'Leary barn is in the upper left area of the map and the map seems to indicate that the fire spread north (to the right) and east from that point.

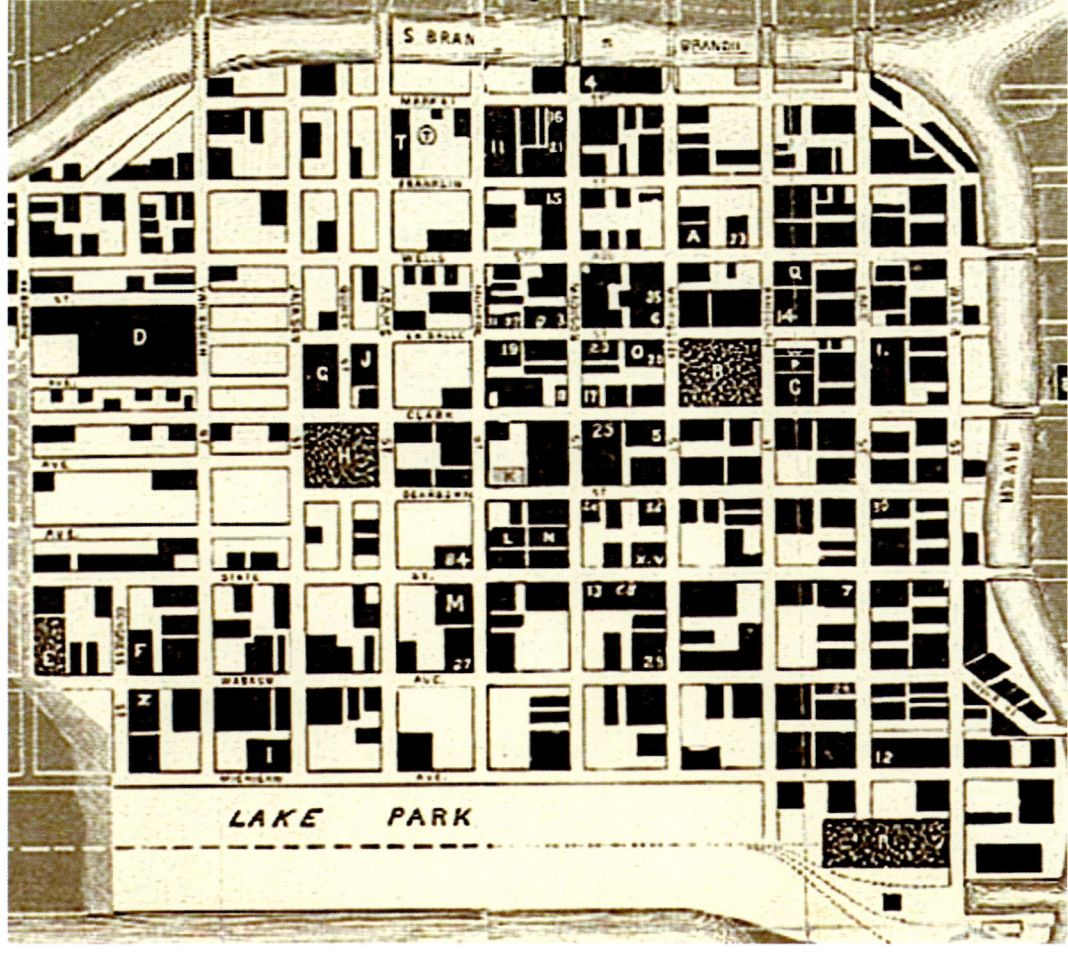

*28 top
Reconstruction
begins. This map,
published by the
Chicago Times in
1872, shows the
first buildings to be
constructed after the
fire (in black), all of
which were made of
stone, brick, or iron.
They include the
Times Building (A),
the Michigan
Central Depot (D),
and the Potter
Palmer's Hotel (M).*

without stopping, from the French Canadian fur trader Louis Joliet and Jesuit missionary Jacques Marquette, to René Robert Cavalier, Monsieur de la Salle, on his way to the Mississippi. The repercussions of the European wars also marked the destiny of the future Chicago. In 1763, in the peace treaty drawn up after the defeat in the Seven Years War, France was forced to give up its possessions in the region to Britain. From the British, the territory became the property of the United States after the War of Independence, and then, in 1803, the US army built Fort

Dearborn, a garrison that was to meet a terrible fate. At the time of the war of 1812, the local natives, in alliance with the British, launched an assault against the settlement and massacred both the soldiers and the settlers in the fort. After the war, Fort Dearborn was rebuilt, but around 1830, Chicago still had no more than 350 inhabitants and was a poverty-stricken village in which only 35 people had the right to vote. The six or seven families of European origin lived alongside groups of half-castes and nomad natives, all in the worst of health. To sum up, it was a rather unappealing

combination of mud, litter, and confusion, as many the passing Englishman wrote.

Chicago made its great leap towards modernity halfway through the nineteenth century, favored by its decisively strategic geographical position for trading exchanges and located as it was at the boundary between the eastern and western regions and the north and south of the North American continent. The construction of the Illinois and Michigan Canal connected the settlement with the banks of the Mississippi, from where it was possible to continue towards the endless western territories. The completion of the connecting wa-

*28 bottom The panic
near Rush Street
bridge in the north of
the city. The original
site of the O'Leary
barn is now the
Chicago firemen's
school.*

*28-29 One of the
terrifying scenes seen
by those first to lend
assistance. The
business district (seen
here from the corner
between State Avenue
and Madison Street)
has been completely
wiped out.*

*29 bottom
A dramatic
illustration on
the cover of The
Illustrated London
News on November
11, 1871. The
inhabitants of
Chicago attempt to
escape from the fire
by fleeing onto
Randolph Street
bridge.*

terway and the arrival of the first railway line in 1848, destined Chicago to be an essential hub of the US transport system. As early as 1855, around a hundred trains each day served the production activities of a population of 60,000 and growing, as a result of a huge wave of immigrants, Irish and German above all.

The development was enormous, sudden, and poorly managed. The terrible hygienic and sanitary conditions of a city in rapid, uncontrolled expansion exacted an increasingly heavy toll. Cholera and smallpox were virtually endemic, at certain periods reaching devastating epidemic proportions. But by now, the in-

significant *Checagou* was being transformed into Chicago. In the new, cyclopic Convention Hall built in 1860, the great assembly of the emerging Republican Party took place, which was to nominate as presidential candidate a virtuous lawyer of great integrity from Illinois. It was on Abraham Lincoln that the heavy burden of the Civil War fell, with the terrible military, political, and economic effort required to keep together a Union rattled by the tempestuous winds of the southern secession. It was the first modern war: a terrible mill of death, blood, hatred, and desperation that swallowed up hundreds of thousands of American lives. Illi-

THE ILLUSTRATED LONDON NEWS.

No. 1678.—VOL. LIX.   SATURDAY, NOVEMBER 11, 1871.   PRICE FIVEPENCE

THE CHICAGO FIRE: THE RANDOLPH-STREET BRIDGE.

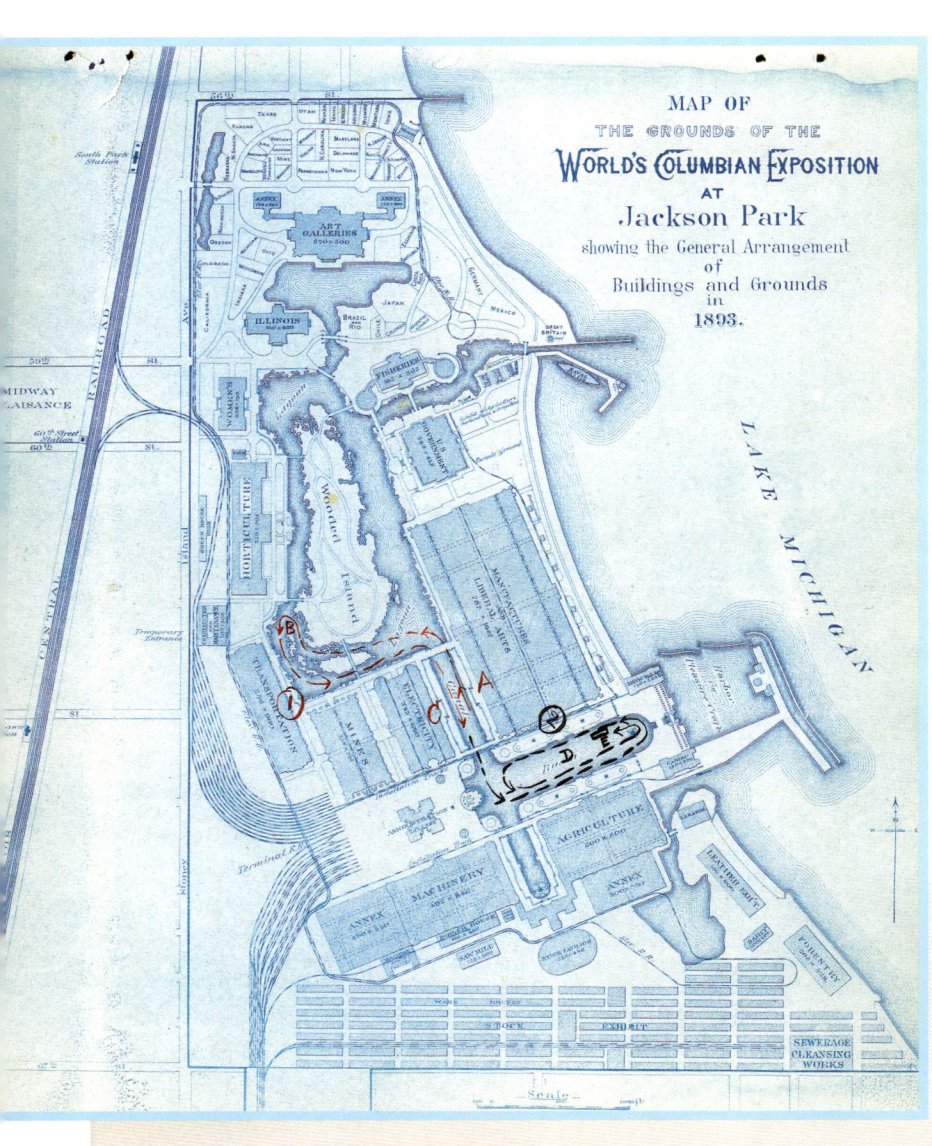

MAP OF
THE GROUNDS OF THE
WORLD'S COLUMBIAN EXPOSITION
AT
Jackson Park
showing the General Arrangement
of
Buildings and Grounds
in
1893.

nois, to honor its loyalty to its illustrious citizen in the White House, took part enthusiastically in the conflict, sending 230,000 men to the front line, 20,000 of them from Chicago. Paradoxically, that tribute of enthusiasm, paid for dearly in the trenches, had been made possible by an extraordinary and extremely modern industrial innovation created to make the life of men happier. In 1847, Cyrus McCormick had invented an ingenious mechanical harvester that took over the work of dozens and dozens of pairs of hands. It was in this way that the agricultural fields of Illinois could be deserted, with their workers sent away to other, much more painful fields, those where the battles were being fought, where thousands of young men were ready to transform themselves into cannon fodder for the sake of northern generals. But after the war, thanks to the products of McCormick, the transport network, and the Union Stockyards containing vast herds of beasts for the industrial production of canned meat, continued to function, allowing the emerging metropolis to become more and more a center for the agricultural business of the western territories.

Chicago still had not completely recovered from the blows dealt to it by the Civil War when it was ravaged by a fire of biblical proportions. It was the fault of Daisy, or Madeline. Or Gwendolyn, depending on who tells the tale. In these parts everybody knows the story of Mrs. O'Leary's cows, except that they still do not agree on the name of the protagonist. The fact is, however, that at nine in the evening on October 8, 1871, Daisy, or Madeline, or Gwendolyn, kicked over a petroleum lamp in the barn of the O'Leary family, setting off the catastrophe, the Great Fire of Chica-

go, which was to destroy the city. The inquest that followed was unable to fully clarify the obscure details of the incident. For some, Mrs. Kate O'Leary confessed in private that she had been present in the barn when the fire broke out, but officially her side of the story was that she had been in bed that night and had not gone to the barn to milk the cows. In the end, the verdict concluded that she played no part in the event and she was not even found negligent. But the decision did not convince everybody and the disputes dragged on for years. It was only on October 7, 1997, exactly 126

30 top The layout of the World's Columbian Exposition: the international fair opened on May 1, 1893 and which represented Chicago's admission to the twentieth century.

30-31 The World's Columbian Exposition earned the city the nickname of the White City for the color of the pavilions built for the occasion and illuminated by large electric lights.

31 top A photograph of the World's Fair by C.D. Arnold was taken in the style of the age from the terrace of the pavilion dedicated to manufacturing and the intellectual arts.

years after the fateful incident in the barn, that the local authorities of Chicago approved a resolution that completely cleared the O'Leary family. Daisy, or Madeline, or Gwendolyn, included.

One of the reasons for this decision is that a theory on the origins of the terrible blaze that at the outset had been rejected as ridiculous and a flight of fantasy is now beginning to be believed. It was suggested that a shower of meteorites struck the entire area and started the initial fire. To back up this theory, it was recalled that the fire that devastated the Pestigo zone in Wisconsin broke out on *that same night*. In the terrible blaze in the forests of Wisconsin, the worst fire ever recorded in the history of the United States, 1,300 people perished and nearly 1,000,000 acres of land were completely destroyed.

Pyromaniac cattle, meteorites, suspicious coincidences, and miscellaneous disputes apart, the Great Fire of Chicago destroyed more than 18,000 buildings, razed 100,000 houses to the ground, carbonized almost 2,000 acres of land and killed nearly 300 people. Chicago was reduced to ashes and incandescent smoking coals, annihilated like Pompeii but still as proud as Carthage. Few landmarks escaped the fury of the flames. The most famous of these is the Water Tower, the elevated water tank that by means of gravity supplied pressure to all the water ducts of the city, and which today is one of its best loved symbols. Built in 1869 to a height of 138 feet, it still stands today, with pride, in the pulsating

heart of Chicago. It is the most illustrious survivor, but not the only one, of the ferocious inferno of 1871. Two religious buildings, the Old St. Patrick's Church of 1856, the oldest church in Chicago, and the Holy Family Church, share this grace and honor. At the time of the fire, Father Damen was in the Holy Family, where he made a vow that he would keep all the votive lamps lit if the church was spared the burning breath of Lu-

cifer. From that moment onwards, the lights of the candles have continued to burn in the quiet semi-darkness of this church. While, almost as if to exorcize the ghosts of the catastrophe, on the exact site of the barn of the O'Leary family, today there stands the Chicago Fire Brigade School where a gilded statue serves as a reminder of the events of those two nights and one day when the city was devoured, quarter after quarter, street after

street, by the jaws of an insatiable dragon. And it was on this empty, virgin sheet of paper, on this laboratory experiment, that the most famous architects of the day began to work. For Chicago, this was an authentic act of fortune.

Right from the first years of its development, the city had had to take the consequences of the mud and unhealthy nature of its territory. For most of the year, the streets were little more than open sewers

and street levels had to be raised at least a dozen times before the Civil War, as the first floors gradually became ground level. Furthermore, as a result of criminal negligance urban waste was being calmly dumped into the Chicago River which ran through the heart of the town. Even the scraps from the industrial butchering operations in the Union Stockyards ended up in the river. Typhoid and cholera had become normal in-habitants of the streets and squares, as was vividly described in the novel by Upton Sinclair, *The Jungle*, published in 1906. The Great Fire of 1871 laid the base for total urban restructuring.

The reconstruction work start-ed immediately, to the tune of a proud, courageous slogan: "*I will.*" It all began with an act of alchemy, the transformation of a poison in-to a medicine. The lush green lakeside which throbs today and underlines the dizzying verticality of the skyscrapers of Chicago owes its existence to one of the most important urban waste dis-posal projects in history. The ruins of the Great Fire were tossed just as they were into the lake, moving Michigan Avenue away from the waterside but auspiciously creat-ing the foundation for that im-mense playground, that place of relaxation, sporting activities, and picnics that attracts millions and

32-33 top The University of Chicago campus as it appeared around 1907. The university was founded in 1890 by the American Baptist Educational Society and by the oil tycoon John D. Rockefeller.

32-33 bottom The city of Chicago on the eve of the 1920s. Before the advent of Hollywood, the city had become the cradle of the silent cinema thanks to stars like Gloria Swanson and Ben Turpin.

HISTORY

34 At the start of the twentieth century the increasingly tall towers in the center of Chicago were aligned with two classic icons of the city skyline, the Tribune Tower (left) and the Wrigley Building (right).

35 top "The City by the Lake": this aerial photograph from 1930 shows the unique appeal of a natural landscape which balances one of the most important modern human settlements.

35 bottom The ingenious vertical garage inaugurated on February 16, 1932 allowed 48 cars to be parked in an area no larger than the space occupied by two cars.

34

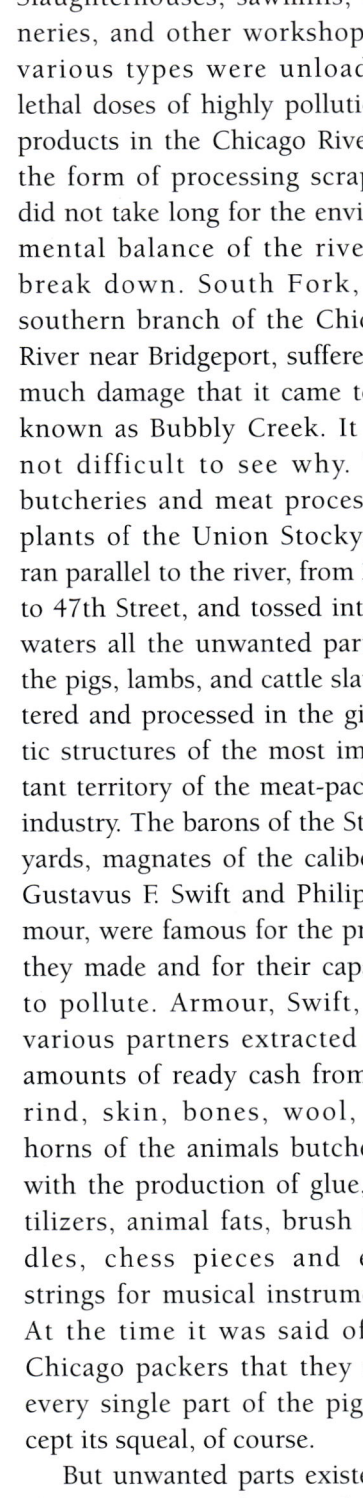

millions of people each year like a magnet.

The whole town was rebuilt, this time with solid, fireproof bricks. In five years, thanks to the reserves accumulated, the commercial soul of Chicago was back on its feet. To be prepared for the challenges of the new century, a very strict fire prevention code was drawn up and no expense was spared in commissioning the most skilled and ingenious architects, those who were most interested in the new wave. In this way, a precedent and a school that was to become an important authority had been set up. From that time onwards, there followed a long series of successes. In 1889, Chicago reached the status of second city in the USA by number of inhabitants. And the nickname of Second City was to stick with it for a long time, until it was overtaken by Los Angeles in this rather disturbing league

table. In 1893, the Columbian Exhibition took place, an international trade fair that achieved extraordinary success and left behind a tangible heritage in two cultural monuments, the Field Museum of Natural History and the Art Institute. It was at this time that the panorama of international architecture added the silhouette of the skyscraper to its repertoire, a modern Tower of Babel launched upwards to exploit vertical rather than horizontal living spaces to the extent that construction techniques and materials technology would permit. But the final crowning moment of that *I will*, announcing the inexorable presence of the skyscraper, took place in 1900, at the dawn of the twentieth century, "the American century" of author John Dos Passos.

As shown, the sudden, powerful, and disorganized development of Chicago did not provide

for careful planning of the urban and industrial waste problems. Slaughterhouses, sawmills, tanneries, and other workshops of various types were unloading lethal doses of highly pollutional products in the Chicago River in the form of processing scrap. It did not take long for the environmental balance of the river to break down. South Fork, the southern branch of the Chicago River near Bridgeport, suffered so much damage that it came to be known as Bubbly Creek. It was not difficult to see why. The butcheries and meat processing plants of the Union Stockyards ran parallel to the river, from 35th to 47th Street, and tossed into its waters all the unwanted parts of the pigs, lambs, and cattle slaughtered and processed in the gigantic structures of the most important territory of the meat-packing industry. The barons of the Stockyards, magnates of the caliber of Gustavus F. Swift and Philip Armour, were famous for the profits they made and for their capacity to pollute. Armour, Swift, and various partners extracted vast amounts of ready cash from the rind, skin, bones, wool, and horns of the animals butchered, with the production of glue, fertilizers, animal fats, brush handles, chess pieces and even strings for musical instruments. At the time it was said of the Chicago packers that they used every single part of the pig, except its squeal, of course.

But unwanted parts existed in abundance, and these ended up on the river bed, where the carcasses slowly and inexorably began to decay. In the course of

for careful planning of the urban and industrial waste problems. Slaughterhouses, sawmills, tanneries, and other workshops of various types were unloading lethal doses of highly pollutional products in the Chicago River in the form of processing scrap. It did not take long for the environmental balance of the river to break down. South Fork, the southern branch of the Chicago River near Bridgeport, suffered so much damage that it came to be known as Bubbly Creek. It was not difficult to see why. The butcheries and meat processing plants of the Union Stockyards ran parallel to the river, from 35th to 47th Street, and tossed into its waters all the unwanted parts of the pigs, lambs, and cattle slaughtered and processed in the gigantic structures of the most important territory of the meat-packing industry. The barons of the Stockyards, magnates of the caliber of Gustavus F. Swift and Philip Armour, were famous for the profits they made and for their capacity to pollute. Armour, Swift, and various partners extracted vast amounts of ready cash from the rind, skin, bones, wool, and horns of the animals butchered, with the production of glue, fertilizers, animal fats, brush handles, chess pieces and even strings for musical instruments. At the time it was said of the Chicago packers that they used every single part of the pig, except its squeal, of course.

time, this crocodile's feast gave up first the fat, which gradually rose to the surface covering it with a thin but compact film, followed by methane gas, which dotted the river with a series of sinister swellings, bubbles that emanated a disgusting stink when they burst. All this was the sadly famous Bubbly Creek.

On Saturday August 1, 1885, a violent storm struck Chicago, forcing the waters of the polluted river beyond all acceptable limits and into Lake Michigan, the reservoir from which the city took its drinking water. While the entire ecosystem suffered devastating blows, from the freshwater fauna to the vegetation of the river, a violent epidemic of cholera and typhoid was unleashed which took a massive toll of victims in the course of a few weeks. Some speak of 90,000 victims, around 12% of the entire population, or one inhabitant in every eight. But some historians question these figures and percentages, being equivalent to those of the Black Death in Europe in the fourteenth century. With statistics in their hands, they considerably reduce the impact of the flood and the poisonous emissions of the Chicago River. Whether or not the figures could be compared with those for the Black Death, the authorities were forced to take action. In 1900, the problem was solved with a decisive and extraordinary effort of hydraulic engineering. The experts from the Metropolitan Sanitary District built a canal that reversed the natural course of the river to remove the polluting load from the lake. Today, the Chicago River enters

HISTORY

36 top *The Gothic architecture of the Tribune Tower built in 1925 stands out like a secular cathedral in the foreground. On the right Michigan Avenue runs northwards towards the John Hancock Center (seen in the background) which dominates the northern boundary of the city.*

36 bottom *The bend of the Chicago River in the heart of the city forms a gentle curve reflected in the glass of 333 West Wacker Building, a 36-floor tower of daring and exclusive design, considered by many to be Chicago's most beautiful building.*

36-37 *Before it becomes the north section of the Magnificent Mile, Michigan Avenue runs parallel to the shoreline beside the city center skyline. They form the two most distinctive features of Chicago.*

legends of the Roaring Twenties, the years in which the fast, confusing growth of organized crime took place. After the Saint Valentine's Day massacre of 1929, when his hired assassins, disguised as policemen, burst into a garage in North Clark Street and shot seven men from the rival gang of Bugs Moran, his fame was ensured. Corrupt mayors and politicians, jazz and blues, personalities from sports and entertainment, agents in the pay of gangsters, bootleggers, speakeasies, gambling, and prostitution: this was the background against which a deadly

the Des Plaines River and the Mississippi, by which it finally reaches the Gulf of Mexico, and the inhabitants of Chicago can proudly say that they taught their river to flow against its own current. *I will…*

On the threshold of the twentieth century, Chicago was flourishing. Before the arrival of Hollywood, it was the cradle of silent cinema, frequented by stars such as Gloria Swanson and Ben Turpin. Patrons, philanthropists, artists, writers and architects had found their place in the sun here. Then came prohibition and the legendary Chicago of the twenties was born. From 1919 to 1933, the town became the property of ruthless gangs who fought each other on the streets from fast cars from which they fired rounds at their rivals from tommy guns, the deadly Thompson machine gun with its round magazine. In this terrifying climate, a fleshy-lipped Italian gangster with deep, pitiless, intelligent eyes, made a name for himself. Al (Alfonso) Capone, also known as Scarface, earned a place for himself in the

36

game of cops and robbers, mobsters and G-men, was played out. Elliot Ness and Al Capone, were portrayed by Kevin Costner and Robert De Niro, in the 1987 film *The Untouchables*. Capone was found guilty of fraud and tax evasion, was sent to Alcatraz and finally died in Miami in 1947, riddled by syphilis. This was how his desparate, violent life met its end, and with it the ended the black legend of the Chicago of the twenties.

On July 15, 1933, Italo Balbo's winged *Centuria* landed in Chicago. This was the squadron of Italian seaplanes that had left Orbetello, on the Tuscan coast, two weeks before. The 99 transatlantic flyers were welcomed enthusiastically by the city. Not even Lindbergh had received such a reception after making the first solo crossing of the Atlantic. The Italian pilots, flying constantly in formation in 24 machines, symbolized the move away from the pioneering to the industrial period of modern aviation. Chicago was selected as the destination as the Exhibition of the Century of Progress was taking place there. Balbo received a hero's welcome, and a street was named after him, Balbo Avenue in the heart of Grant Park, which still bears his name today. He was even crowned a chief of the Sioux by an elderly member of that Indian nation, who placed a ceremonial headdress on his head. He had become an improbable 'flying eagle'. After the war, the first US ambassador from the democratic, antifascist Italy, Alberto Tarchiani, asked the mayor of Chicago to change the embarrassing name of the street, which referred to one of the men most admired and esteemed during the Fascist regime.

The reply was, "Why? Wasn't Balbo the man who flew across the Atlantic?" Whether or not this was politically correct, Chicago had no intention of denying that it had had the honor of receiving the Italian transatlantic flyers. The city confirmed its place in the avant-garde of the modern world and progress, in every field. On December 2, 1942, the first nuclear chain reaction took place in a university laboratory and it's here that more than half the radar equipment used by the US armed forces was manufactured. In 1995, the magazine *Fortune* wrote

that Chicago was the most exciting city in the United States.

This is also the headquarters of the huge and formidable Democratic Party machine, in a tradition of power that began with the mayor Edward J. Kelly, who stayed in office for four terms, from 1933 to 1947, and then continued with the Daley family dynasty. From Richard J. Daley, with his six terms (1955-1975) to Richard Daley II, this was an administration that organized to perfection the typically American mechanism of the spoil system, a euphemism which simply means

'winner takes all.' The technocrats of the Daley family have oiled and continue to oil the mechanisms of the Democratic machine. And you have to be a really class act in a city like Chicago, where politics is one of the strongest passions, together with beer and sport. These passions up to not so long ago had an unmistakable temple, the tavern. Yes, the tavern, not the bar, was the preferred location for the celebration of elections, Michael Jordan and his Bulls, or the gridiron successes of the gigantic Chicago Bears, the local football

team that have been champions several times.

This is another of the reasons why the Chicago of today is a metropolis with a unique and unmistakable fascination, irrespective of the pedantic, problematical league tables. In its own inimitable way, it casts its glance from the antichamber of the Great Plains, the vast horizontal spaces of the West, to another dimension, which is the vertical in all its extremes. It is a dense network of quarters containing nearly three million inhabitants, living around the focal point of the center, The Loop con-

taining a huge ethnic palette of a thousand colors and a thousand neighborhoods, including Irish, Africans, Poles, Germans, Italians, Greeks, Russians, Swedes, and Turks, now joined by Cambodians, Puerto Ricans, Japanese, Chinese, Arabs, and Jews. There is an emotional climate where the flavors are strong, hard, crude, dynamic, and efficient.

With cosmopolitan fabric *par excellence*, Chicago is a center of culture and journalism, boasting numerous publications from *Esquire* to *Science Digest*, to the glamour of *Chicago* to the black

pride of *Ebony*. Journalists have expressed the miseries and splendors of the profession from the pages of the *Chicago Daily News,* in successful comedies such as *Front Page,* or from correspondents the *Chicago Tribune* such as William Shirer, who described the intricacies behind the scenes of the Third Reich. Ernst Hemingway, Thornton Wilder, Louis Armstrong, Gene Krupa, Benny Goodman, and Mahalia Jackson can all be linked to Chicago. A special relationship with culture, art, and literature exists here, which explains initiatives that would otherwise be difficult to understand. Towards the end of August 2001, the *New York Times* published news of a curious position taken up by the mayor of Chicago. "Silence, please. Chicago's reading, everybody's reading the same book at the same time," was the authoritative newspaper's headline. Richard Daley had de-

cided to ask the inhabitants of the town to read more and spend less time every day hypnotized in front of the TV. The book he chose was one of the masterpieces of US literature, Harper Lee's *To Kill a Mockingbird*, which won the Pulitzer Prize in 1961. He told the public libraries – in which it's in third place in the list of the most widely read novels of all time – to purchase 5,000 copies and encouraged the bookshops to display it proudly in their windows. The success was enormous, and within only a few days all the copies had gone, which proves that there's more to Chicago than just skyscrapers.

The sweat of the factories no longer produces a quarter of the economic power of the United States of America, amid environmental pollution and social Darwinism. But Chicago, The Big Onion, remains, together with its proud motto, *I will….*

38-39 The Navy Pier in the 1980s before it was rebuilt has became one of Chicago's best-loved locations. The purification plants stand next to the structure.

39 The Navy Pier today is framed by Chicago's two best-known buildings: the Sears Tower to the south and the "Big John" of the Hancock Center to the north.

40 top The Navy Pier and Lake Point Tower before recent work altered the city layout.

40 bottom This is how the area appeared after reopening in 1995 following construction that cost almost 200 million dollars. It now includes a

museum for children, restaurants, a shopping mall, and a giant Imax cinema screen plus, of course, the panoramic wheel the height of a six story building.

41 top The business district of Chicago bounded to the north by the John Hancock Center before the convulsive growth of the 1990s.

41 bottom The renovation of this part of Chicago is summarized by the State of Illinois Center (bottom left) and a forest of new skyscrapers.

42-43 Recreated on the ashes of its former self, today Chicago is one of America's cities with the largest number of ethnic communities (here we see one of the city suburbs).

44-45 The shoreline, skyscrapers, and tourist port crammed with boats, beaches, golf courses, and tennis courts are all part of the Lakefront. This area has aspects of the ideal city of the twenty first century, with 25 miles of gardens and parks.

46-47 Lines stretch away into the distance in the dark illuminated by the pulsing energy of lights and colors: a night filled with a million individual stories that go towards making up the weave and weft of Chicago. It is all in the spirit of "E pluribus unum," as the motto of the United States says.

GRANT

PARK

Urbs in horto, the city in a garden, is one of the mottoes of Chicago. It should come as no surprise to learn that the Chicago Park District is one of the most important municipal departments in the world. It manages over 7,000 acres of public green space culminating in Grant Park, the jewel in the crown of the entire system. Covering several blocks alongside the Loop, on the shores of the lake bordered by Michigan Avenue to the west, Randolph Street to the north, and Roosevelt Road to the south, it is an explosion of lawns where millions of occasional visitors and locals meet each summer. Designed in the twenties by Daniel Burnham, inspired by the gardens of Versailles (or at least so they say), the area arose from nothing out of the rubble left behind by the Great Fire of Chicago that had been dumped into Lake Michigan. Today the Buckingham Fountain, in spite of the British overtones of its name, evokes the splendor of the waterworks of Versailles, proudly showing off its three basins finely cut out of pink marble, each resting on the one

50-51 Grant Park is Chicago's pride and joy, a green oasis where millions of Chicagoans and visitors flock each summer to enjoy the open air shows and the music festival. The photograph shows the Field Museum of Natural History (left) and the Shedd Aquarium (right), two of the city's best known and most popular attractions.

51 top The skyscrapers, like the Sears Tower, in the city center seem to look down on the hotels that face onto Grant Park and the port of the Chicago Yacht Club.

51 bottom Chicago's greenest area is one of the hubs of city life. Here we see the northeast section surrounded by skyscrapers like the Carbide&Carbon Building and the Illinois Center.

53 bottom This photograph looks toward the north side of the park and shows the buildings that make up the Chicago Cultural Center and, on the right, the Carbide&Carbon Building. In the background it is possible to make out the Chicago Teather District.

below, escorted by four pairs of Cyclopic bronze seahorses. A baroque, imperial setting for 133 jets of water that shoot up to around 130 feet, it recycles, 400,000 gallons of water, fueling triumphal geysers that celebrate the start and end of summer from May to October. Behind this fountain is a view of the boldest and most towering profiles of the center, in fascinating architectural perspective which lights up in magical colors by night, behind the effervescent spray of the imposing cascades of water.

In Grant Park from early May to the end of October, the exhibition of bronze statues by contemporary artists has become a welcome tradition. Throughout the summer, the park is transformed into an open air theater where extremely popular festivals and concerts take place one after another in the picnic areas and the expertly tended gardens, from the softball fields to the Petrillo Music Shell, where the Chicago Blues Festival takes place every June. This concert series first took place in 1983, the year when Muddy Waters died. Today, the most famous blues musicians in the country take part, attracting bigger and bigger crowds each year. Grant Park also saw the bubbling over of the tensions produced by the Vietnam war, when student protests during the 1968 Democratic Convention were violently countered by police on the order of the mayor, Richard Daley.

The park also contains some of

52 In 1871 the Great Fire raged through Chicago for two nights and a day, razing it to the ground. Nouvelle vague's architects created new and innovative urban designs on the fresh

sheet that was the site of the city while the rubble from the terrible fire was taken to the shores of Lake Michigan to create new land. This is where Grant Park now lies onto which some of the

most important and famous buildings in the city face, for example, the Auditorium and the Santa Fe (in the photograph) that stands behind the building that is home to the Art Institute.

53 top Designed in the 1920s by Burnham, Grant Park has become one of Chicago's best-loved and cared for areas. It is surrounded on three sides by old buildings standing close together, and by modern skyscrapers.

the most interesting and well known museums in the city. The Art Institute, for example, displays its extraordinary collection of paintings and sculptures located in a series of Neo-Classical buildings built for the World's Columbian Exposition of 1893. The bronze lions at the entrance from South Michigan Avenue have become one of the most photographed sights in the city. The John G. Shedd Aquarium faces the shores of Lake Michigan, and its Neo-Classical facade invites visitors into the biggest covered aquarium in the world. It hosts more than 6,000 marine creatures representing over 700 species from all the world's seas, such as those from the splendid Caribbean Barrier Reef displayed in an artificial sliver of ocean immersed in 90,000 gallons of water. Opposite, in the Field Museum of Natural History, with a chilling smile of welcome, stands Sue, the biggest and most complete skeleton of *Tyrannosaurus Rex* ever discovered, while under the dome of the Adler Planetarium the secrets of astronomy are revealed by means of the most modern learning technologies.

55 bottom A gift to the city by Kate Sturges Buckingham, opened in 1927 in the center of Grant Park, it was the largest decorative fountain in the world. When the wind in the Windy City blows, the Buckingham Fountain can turn into a sort of giant firehose that soaks unfortunate passers-by. On summer nights, its jets are illuminated with colored lights that are reflected on the windows of the downtown skyscrapers.

54-55 and 54 bottom Buckingham Fountain consists of three pink marble basins on top of one another gazed upon by four pairs of bronze cyclopic sea horses. This Baroque form is the setting for 133 computer-controlled jets of water that spurt 11,000 gallons of water into the air each minute.

56

56 top Since 1930, more than 100 million people have visited the John G. Shedd Aquarium, the largest covered aquarium in the world. It holds 8,000 examples of salt and freshwater life including beluga whales, sharks, turtles, rays, alligators, pirañas, penguins, and a fantastic reproduction of a part of the Amazon River basin.

56-57 The Field Museum of Natural History has few rivals in the world. It is also home to Sue, the largest and most complete Tyrannosaurus Rex ever found.

57 top The Adler Planetarium was built in 1928 thanks to the munificence of Max Adler who donated one million dollars to the city for it to be built.

57 bottom Soldier Field is the stadium where the Chicago Bears play, the city's football team. Built in 1925 and rebuilt in 1971, it can hold more than 100 thousand fans.

58-59 The entire Lakefront area (with 600 parks, 30 or so beaches, and ocean-going sailing and motorboats) was designed to offer the widest variety of recreational activities possible to the public, including jogging, skating, and cycling. Cycling magazines have placed Chicago among the top ten cities in the United States for cycling.

But it is in the nearby Soldier Field that we encounter the most incredible explosion of flags, furore, sweat, and enthusiasm of all the sports played in Chicago. In this 120,000-plus capacity stadium, with its colonnades that recall Ancient Roman coliseums, the gladiators of today can be seen in crash helmets and shoulder pads, the heroes of American football.

The favorite local team is the Bears, winners of their first and last Superbowl in 1985, the mythical championship final that has the entire population of the United States, the president included, glued to their TV screens. Every game on the shores of Lake Michigan is transformed into a joyous, wildly colored festival of fans and sport.

60-61 This is the Chicago Marina. Chicago has several nicknames: Urbs in horto, The City that Works, City of Big Shoulders, Second City, as well as the well-known Windy City. The winds that blow off Lake Michigan are constant and much appreciated by sailors but can become very violent.

 # THE LOOP

For some, it is the clattering monster that passes their houses at bedroom height, a metropolitan nightmare halfway between *Doctor Mabuse's Cabinet* and *Blade Runner*. For others, it is one of the best loved symbols of the city, a romantic, well-meaning dragon whose sinuous tail glows golden when it is bathed in the soft light of sunset. In the heart of the city, the underground rail system, maybe envious of the vertical sweep of the skyscrapers, emerges and rises up towards the sky. But before it gets there, it is forced to curb its ambitions and continue around a circuit that seems to have no end. The Chicago Elevated Train System, or "The El" as its known in the local parlance, is closed downtown within an elevated loop, which has inspired the nick-name of the city center, The Loop, evoking ima-

ges worthy of Tolkein, much in fashion today. Roughly speaking, the limits of this vital nerve center are bounded to the north and west by the Chicago River, to the east by Grant Park, which runs along Michigan Avenue, and to the south by the Congress Parkway.

This is where we find the skyscrapers that have contributed to the history of Chicago and US architecture, from the prototypes of the late nineteenth century to the last jewels designed by Mies van der Rohe. They say that they were built to resolve the space problems of a horizontal metropolis by directing it towards the vertical. But there are some who say that this determination to climb up to the skies is a kind of emotional retaliation, a mental and perhaps unconscious effort to redeem the origins of a city rooted and planted in the earth like an onion, just li-

ke that *Checagou* of the Algonquins from which it takes its name.

Whatever the reason, the most widely accepted version says that it was the escalation of prices in the struggle to acquire land in the center that led owners to make the most of the space

available. The new technology available, construction materials, and electric power for the lifts, enabled architects to discover the obvious solution: to think and build vertically. The swampy terrain forced them to face new challenges and find new solutions, as the structures of the

64 The Chicago Loop is dominated by the Sears Tower, the city's most famous skyscraper. It was in Chicago during the 1880s that the concept of the skyscraper was born for reasons of aesthetics and economic convenience.

65 top A low level flight over downtown. We see the Amoco Building (Chicago's second tallest building) and Two Prudential Plaza with its tapered and pointed roof.

65 bottom The profile of the Loop: from the left we see (among others) the Amoco Building, Two Prudential Plaza, the Theater District, and the Sears Tower.

earlier concrete skyscrapers placed huge loads on their foundations. Consequently, walking the central streets today, looking at the juxtaposition of the earliest and latest species of skyscraper, from those built after the Great Fire of 1871 to the steel structures of today, is like leafing through a book on the history of urban engineering and watching the rapid evolution of construction techniques unfold before our eyes. Among other reasons, this is because the concept of the skyscraper has changed dramatically in only a few decades. Today we think in terms of buildings with more than 100 floors, higher than three football fields. But one of the first in the series, the Montauk Building, now demolished, filled the horizon of Chicago with no more than 10 floors, an almost incredible height for those times. Etched onto these Chicago landmarks are the signatures of the most famous architects of the day, William Le Baron Jenney, Louis Sullivan, and Daniel Burnham.

We owe The Rookery, built in 1886, a combination of romantic, Gothic, Moorish, and Venetian details bringing together the old and the new to Burnham and his partner John Wellborn Root. The spacious lobby was then restored

66 bottom left and 67 The Amoco Building and Two Prudential Plaza stand out in the forest of skyscrapers in the heart of Chicago. They are very special. The *first was designed in 1973 inspired by the linearity of the Twin Towers in New York. The second is from 1990 and harks back to the Neo-Gothic lines fashionable in the 1930s.*

66 right The building at 150 North Michigan Avenue is unmistakable with its 45° sloping roof. It was built in 1984 on the north corner of Grant Park.

68 The area of Chicago known as The Loop is named after the path of the elevated metropolitan train that circles downtown and the main buildings in the commercial center. The Elevated Train System rings the heart of Chicago where the alternation of modern and "old" buildings mirrors the urban stratification that took place during the twentieth century.

68-69 The Chicago Theater District and the Daley Center (in the foreground) occupy the north section of The Loop. On the left we see the rugged silhouette of 150 North Michigan Building and on the extreme right, the Neo-Gothic spire of the Chicago Temple.

and corrected by Frank Lloyd Wright to give The Rookery a new soul, an austere facade with a sumptuous entrance hall, in the style of the Chicago School: very linear on the outside with gold and marble interiors, giving a beautiful but functional architectural effect. Less than a block away is the Chicago Board of Trade, for many years the highest building in the city, an Art Deco tower surmounted by a stainless steel statue of Ceres, the Roman

god of the harvest. It is in this building that around half the grain and maize produced throughout the world is bought, sold, and then distributed to the tables of the planet. Not far away, to emphasize the strategic and financial importance of The Loop, is the Chicago Mercantile Exchange, where precious metals, foreign currency, and miscellaneous resources pass from hand to hand at a rate of 50 billion dollars a day.

In the same area is the Manhattan Building, built by Jenney in 1890. It may not be the finest but it is undoubtedly the first of the city's skyscrapers to be built with a steel outer casing, the link in the chain and the direct ancestor of the modern skyscraper. Then there is the Monadnock Building, designed and built by Burnham & Root in 1891. The highest office building of its time, with concrete walls 5.9 feet thick, it challenged the wind and

the lightning of the skies. But it is at the northern edge of the Loop, at 333 West Wacker Drive, that we find an incredible architectural wedge, for many the most beautiful building in Chicago. With a facade that follows the bend in the Chicago River with a fantastic glass wall, soft and curved, it rests, dignified and solid, on the corner of the street.

It takes a lot of walking to reach the impressive, unmistakable profile of the Sears Tower, the

highest building in the world until 1997, when it was controversially overtaken by the Petronas Towers of Kuala Lumpur. It stands 1454 feet high, with 110 floors and a hundred or so lifts, one of which leads to the Skydeck Observatory in less than 70 seconds, affording a breathtaking, eagle's eye view. On a clear, breezy day, you can see four states from here, Illinois, Michigan, Wisconsin, and Indiana, the real triumph of the Chicago School.

70 This photograph shows the north corner of The Loop enclosed by the Chicago River. The system of bridges that connects the western and downtown areas of the city is clearly seen. Note the two octagonal towers of the Chicago Mercantile Exchange Center in the foreground. Where South Branch and North Branch of the Chicago River meet it is possible to make out the innovative profile of 333 West Wacker. In the center of the photograph there is the area around City Hall and the Theater District and towards the top of the image, the Magnificent Mile.

71 The north corner of The Loop where the two branches of the Chicago River meet. Among the more unusual buildings, there are 333 and 225 W. Wacker, the innovative cone section of the James R. Thompson Center and, on the far right, the green roofed Title & Trust Center.

72 The antithetical but complementary silhouettes of the Amoco Building and Two Prudential Plaza dominate the eastern section of The Loop on the boundary of Grant Park.

73 Fifteen years passed between the construction of the Amoco Building and that of Two Prudential Plaza. The lines of the two buildings demonstrate the time gap. The pure verticality of the gigantic Amoco Building was inspired by the same design philosophy as the World Trade Center in New York. The architect of the other preferred to reconsider the aesthetic elements that typified skyscrapers during the dawn of the twentieth century.

76 and 77 top In the middle of the pointed forest in The Loop, there are a number of buildings that are rather incongruous, for example the Harold Washington Library Center (the second largest public library in the world after the British Library in London).

77 bottom left The 1926 Jewelers Building (later named the Pure Oil Building) was the location of many of the world's great jewelers. Gigantic lifts carried customers' cars to the upper floors.

77 bottom right At 568 feet high, the Chicago Temple is the tallest Neo-Gothic church in the world. It was completed in 1923.

78 and 79 *Chicago's urban transport system, the El, runs in a loop through the heart of the center in a rectangle bounded by Wabash Avenue, Lake Street, Wells Street, and Van Buren Street. The city's geographical center lies at the junction of State and Madison Street and is known as "ground zero." This is the point from which the numbering of the blocks and buildings begins, increasing by 100 on each block. If you can see the central point on a city map, it is easy to find any address you wish.*

80 and 81 For years the Sears Tower was the tallest building in the world. It was built by Sears Roebuck & Co. and was officially opened in 1974 after just three years of work. The tower stands 1454 feet high and has 110 floors. It is formed by 74,000 tons of steel divided into nine juxtaposed cubes that taper as they rise and which are separated at the 49th, 66th, and 90th floors. The building was designed to resist the high winds which, in the Windy City, is an important factor to bear in mind. Its sides have 16,000 windows which are washed eight times a year using special machinery. Roughly 1.5 million visitors ride to the Skydeck at the top of the building each year to enjoy the glorious view.

82 bottom left
The photograph was taken at the point where the two branches of the Chicago River meet. On the right we see 333 and on the left 225 West Wacker Drive. The former was completed in 1983 in a triangular layout, while the latter, in Postmodern style and characterized by a roof with four large skylights, was opened six years later.

82 top right The R.R. Donnely Building was designed in 1992 by the Catalan architect Ricardo Bofill in Neo-Classical style. The proportional lines and marble elements are reminiscent of Latin and Hellenic architecture.

83 The unmistakable roof of 150 North Michigan Avenue slopes at a 45° angle on the north corner of Grant Park. The skyscraper is one of the most original designs in Chicago and was completed in 1984.

84-85 The water of
the Chicago River
and Lake Michigan
meet east of The
Loop. An impressive
system of bridges
allows the central
section of the
city–a sort of
island–to remain
in communication
with the northern
and western
districts.

84 bottom and 85 With the implementation in 1900 of an extraordinary hydraulic system, the engineer Rudolph Hering solved the problem of the pollution of the Chicago River, which had been the source of the city's environmental problems. A canal was dug that inverted the natural course of the river and thereby carried the polluting materials away from the lake. Today the Chicago River flows into the Des Plaines River and the Mississippi from where it eventually reaches the Gulf of Mexico. The inhabitants of the Big Onion are therefore able to claim that their river flows backwards.

86 top and 87 The Chicago River and its bridges are a well-known feature of the North American city. The history of Chicago's bascule bridges is recounted in the State Street Bridge Gallery. The rivers that flow out of Lake Michigan contributed to the great leap to modernity that Chicago made during the mid-nineteenth century when it was considered an essential hub of the American transportation system.

86 bottom Michigan Avenue Bridge connects The Loop to the northeast section of Chicago where the Magnificent Mile begins. It was completed on two levels in 1920.

89 *A very rainy city, Chicago has wet but not overly cold winters. The picture shows a rainy day with a morning haze wrapping the downtown skyscrapers.*

90-91 *Lying in the Central Time Zone, Chicago has almost 3 million inhabitants. Chicagoland is the term used to identify the suburbs that surround the city to the west, north, and south and which bring the total population up to 8 million. But the receptive capability of the city is extraordinary if you consider that it receives about 30 million visitors each year, putting it in third place behind Las Vegas and New Orleans.*

88 *For 24 years the Sears Tower was the tallest building in the world until the Petronas Towers were constructed in Kuala Lumpur. At 1,480 feet and 88 floors tall, the Malaysian constructions stole the record from Chicago's building but … should the aerials be included? With its tall aerials, the Sears Tower reaches a height of 1,700 feet. The debate is still open and opinions divided.*

THE

MAGNIFICENT

MILE

Glamorous North Michigan Avenue is an urban Grand Canyon with glass and marble walls, a major road that runs straight as a ramrod over its route and history. This is the Magnificent Mile, the Chicago strip, another of its typical, distinctive symbols, one mile of refined, exclusive shopping which includes three vertical malls with more than two hundred boutiques and shops, cinemas, restaurants, and bookshops. The parade of shop windows seems like a Hollywood bazaar, with gold, silver, jewels, deluxe footwear, and signed fashions, a combination of the Abu Dhabi duty free shop, Milan's fashionable clothing shops, and Rodeo Drive.

The first milestone in this journey into luxury and extravagance starts at the Wrigley Building, and maybe it could not have been otherwise. Here, in 1779, Jean-Baptiste Point du Sable built his hut alongside the future site of one of the symbolic buildings of Chicago. Thanks above all to the rather gloomy clocktower, for many years this structure has been one of the most famous and clearly recognized urban icons, born in the days of the Wrigley empire of chewing gum. Along the Magnificent Mile, we travel on a journey through the history of the city's development, starting in the twenties, when the construction of the Michigan Avenue Bridge made it necessary to find new space to the north of the Chicago River. Here in 1922, the Tribune Tower was built, the "castle" in Neo-Gothic style

where Colonel Robert McCormick defended himself with his deadly paper cannons loaded with ink. He was the all-powerful editor of the most important local daily, the Chicago Tribune. It was in this building that the emotional articles of Ring Lard-

ner, passionate bard of the city's slums, first saw the light of day. By night, both the Wrigley Building and the Tribune Tower are lit up from the bridge, bringing into cold, pitiless relief these two symbols of US power. The shadows are flattened, as if under the

lights of the TV cameras, and the more the buildings are lit up the more they seem unreal.

In the heart of North Michigan Avenue there also beats the pulse of the unshakeable Water Tower, a symbol of Chicago's resistance to adversity. This hy-

94 The John Hancock Center dominates the northeastern areas of Chicago from a height of 1,127 feet. In the foreground, at "only" 870 feet, stands the highly original 900 North Michigan Avenue Building with its four lanterns that illuminate the night sky of the Magnificent Mile with a magical light.

95 Crossing Michigan Avenue Bridge from The Loop, you enter the dazzling heart of the Magnificent Mile, Chicago's most famous "street." The picture was taken looking down on some of the cross streets of the Magnificent Mile: from the right we see the Riverwalk, Illinois Street, Grand Avenue, and Ohio Avenue. The buildings include (from the right) the Wrigley Building (on the bank of the Chicago River), the Tribune Tower with its banner, the NBC Tower, and the black silhouette of the Lake Point Tower.

96 Chicago is home to 40 or so of the top 500 corporations listed by Fortune magazine each year. The economic life of the city pulses in its skyscrapers. In this feverish scenario, such buildings are considered by some to be modern temples. In some cases, they even bear an aesthetic resemblance to churches: look at the Neo-Gothic design of the Wrigley Building and the Tribune Tower (top and right) or the slender bell-tower of the Water Tower (bottom left) squeezed between "real" skyscrapers.

97 The Magnificent Mile is an urban Grand Canyon dedicated to commerce while also being the legacy of a tradition. It was close to this area in 1779 that Jean-Baptiste Point du Sable built his trading post, in the nucleus of what was to become modern Chicago. Today the most famous symbols of that epoch are the majestic John Hancock Center and the Water Tower with its annex WT Place, a shopping center with more than 150 selected outlets.

draulic lung of the city refused to give in to the Great Fire of 1871, and in the face of so much courageous tenacity it was labeled with the rather banal and disappointing description of "a monstrosity" by Oscar Wilde during his visit to the city in 1882. Even though it is only a more or less elegant cover of a water tank at the top of a pole, it remains one of the important landmarks of Chicago. And it is not by chance that its name has been given to one of the best known shopping malls in town.

But the building that literally dominates the panorama of the Magnificent Mile is Big John, otherwise known as the John Hancock Center, an ultramodern steel and smoked glass stalactite of 100 floors. At 1,127 feet high, only the Sears Tower looks down on it. From the observatory on the 94th floor, according to a highly reliable survey among locals, the view from here is much better than from its taller brother, even though the latter has nine floors more. The best time is at

sunset, when the sun from the west immerses the entire city in the fiery blaze of its goodbye. In the last skyscraper in this adventure in the Big Onion, all that remains to do is to pay a visit to the highest restaurant in the Midwest.

98 and 99 The building that dominates the view of the Magnificent Mile and all the North Side of Chicago is Big John, i.e. the John Hancock Center, an amazing stalactite of steel and smoked glass which, at 1,127 feet tall and with 100 floors, is second only to the Sears Tower. Big John stands on Michigan Avenue which runs parallel to Lake Michigan on the west side of the building and is the most exclusive, sophisticated, and complete shopping area in the city. With its cyclopean aerials, it seems to want to reach even higher, to literally scrape the sky.

100-101 This is a view of Michigan Avenue aligned with Big John. All around, like ranks of medieval vassals, stand the slender profiles of the city center skyscrapers.

102-103 At dusk, the Magnificent Mile is lit up by the evening traffic and a long strip of inviting shop windows that make a walk through the heart of Chicago a pleasant relaxation for visitors, their faces pointing upwards to appreciate the flight of vertical lines sculpted in steel that change color as they ascend toward the sky. The photograph was taken from Water Tower Place.

104 top The blue roof of 690 Lake Shore Place is terminated by four turrets and a lantern. Its Gothic-Victorian design is from the 1920s.

104 bottom Skimming over Park Tower towards The Loop, we see the massive silhouette of the Merchandising Mart in the upper section of the photograph. It contains more than 3,230,000 square feet of shops and is thought to be the largest shopping center in the world.

105 At the foot of the John Hancock Center stands the unmistakable and no less-loved Water Tower, a tiny "skyscraper" built in 1869 by William Boyington to provide water to the city's houses. The water tank managed to resist the flames of the Great Fire of 1871.

106 The two large and uncommon cylinders that rise into the sky belong to the Marina City Complex designed by Bertrand Goldberg. Their unusual shape has led to them being nicknamed "twin corncobs."

107 top The Magnificent Mile, The Loop and, in general, all of Chicago is a busy construction site. Skyscrapers like the one in the photograph, in Kinzie Street, rise each year at striking speed.

107 bottom The Magnificent Mile, Chicago's strip, is one of the top five shopping areas of the world. A straight line made up of glass windows, marble, and glamor runs for a mile offering refined shops and even three vertical malls with more than 200 boutiques, shops, cinemas, restaurants, and bookshops. Characteristic and exclusive buildings are to be found in this area, including the Marriott Hotel (left) and 900 Michigan Avenue (right, of which we only see two of the four roof lanterns).

108-109 The twin problems of traffic and parking have found an innovative and brilliant solution in the lower section of the twin corncobs.

110-111 The northwest district of The Loop at dusk. This is where the skyscrapers stand that have forged the history of Chicago and international architecture, from the prototypes from the end of the nineteenth century to the last works by Miles van der Rohe. Today it is one of the best-known and most beautiful skylines in the world.

THE

LAKEFRONT

114-115 Three pictures taken from Lake Michigan give three different profiles of the Lakefront, the green coastal strip that stretches for almost 25 miles and covers 74,133 acres of public parkland. Urbs in horto, the city in a garden, is one of Chicago's best-loved nicknames. The beaches that line Lake Michigan within the city limits are protected areas "open, clear, and free." Oak Street Beach, at the start of Lincoln Park, north of the Navy Pier and lining Lake Shore Drive, is perhaps the loveliest of the almost 600 public parks in Chicago. This is where Lincoln Park Zoo can be found, the most popular zoo in the country, with its gigantic 130,000-square feet wide greenhouse built in 1891 to contain hundreds of examples of flora and fauna from all over the world.

It is about 25 miles long and the best thing to do is walk, but if you've got neither the time nor the will, a bicycle does just as well. Chicago is built on the shore of Lake Michigan, the only one in the Great Lakes system that is 100% in the USA, Yankee through and through. Along Lake Shore Drive, one of the most congested roads in town, history runs, architecture is mirrored, and you can breathe in the soul of Chicago. Gliding towards the city, the tormented, pointed architecture of the center anticipates the distant natural barrier of the Rockies, which interrupt the endless monotony of the Great Plains to announce the immensity of the Pacific Ocean beyond the spiny ridges and the snow-capped peaks. Chicago is a summing up and an anticipation of what lies beyond the western frontiers, promise, adventure, dreams, hopes, mystery, and torment. On the one hand there is the lake, which brings the frigid breath of the northern winds. On the other, a narcissistic mirror of steel and glass reflects the glimmering of the sun on the waves. In the middle stretches a long strip of parks and gardens, one of the best loved and most famous reminders of Daniel H. Burnham.

In 1909, the prestigious architect persuaded the local administration to accept his project for the city. At least 20 miles along the shores of Lake Michigan had to be set aside exclusively for public green areas. It is thanks to him, his foresight and charisma, that today it is possible to experience the Lakefront Trail, over 18 miles closed to traffic, and frequented by passers-by, joggers, cyclists, and skaters in search of relaxation and healthy contact with nature. The area between McCormick Place and Hyde Park to the south is considered dangerous, which explains the presence of gigantic policemen on mountain bikes. There are around thirty beaches along the shores of the lake, monitored by athletic lifeguards throughout the summer. You could almost get the impression that you've parachuted onto the burning sands of one of the most popular sea resorts of America, especially at Oak Street

THE LAKEFRONT

Beach, at the start of the so-called Gold Coast, not by coincidence nicknamed the Saint Tropez of the Midwest. However the summer is short, and with the arrival of winter there blows a wind that brings the howls of the arctic wolves in its wake. But Chicago owes its nickname of The Windy City not so much to the howling gales as to the fact that the promoters of the Columbian Exhibition of 1893 exasperated the rest of the country by obsessively crying the marvels of the city and its international trade fair to the four winds.

Oak Street Beach is at the start of Lincoln Park, which is perhaps the finest of the 600 public green areas in Chicago. In the heart of the protected area is the Lincoln Park Zoo, which attracts more visitors than any other in the USA. The Victorian elegance of the buildings that house almost 2,000 animals reduces, as much as possi-

116 Breakfast is served on the roof of a skyscraper on Lake Shore Drive, where one can enjoy the sun and the view, and, if the weather permits, take a dip in the pool. 116-117 Lake Shore Drive runs down the side of the city, crossing many splendid urban landscapes and several large parks. On the left we see the Navy Pier and the unmistakable clover-shaped Lake Point Tower. The Amoco Building and Two Prudential Plaza stand in the center of the photograph. The Sears Tower can be seen in the background.

ble, the sadness caused by seeing elephants, a variety of primates, polar bears, and other beasts shut up in cages. Much happier are the nearly 130,000 square feet of the giant greenhouse built in 1891 to offer tropical scenarios with hundreds of examples of flora and fauna from all over the world.

With Lake Michigan and the skyscrapers, 600 public parks, thirty or so beaches, the tourist harbor crowded with boats of all shapes and sizes, golf courses and tennis courts, Chicago shows some of the typical features of the ideal city of the twenty-first century. Add the electricity of the business quarter and the nervous anxiety of the stock exchange negotiations that decide the fate of the world economy, this bustling metropolis is constantly struggling with the present in the rush to grasp hold of the problems of tomorrow. Chicago can boast 600 public parks, some 30 beaches, and harbors for sailing and motor boats. This is Chicago, where basketball and football are taken seriously, politics is a pastime, and where blues, jazz, and hot dogs can be found on the shores of one of the widest lakes in North America.

118-119 The Chicago River mixes with Lake Michigan. To the left there is The Loop, the heart of the city, in the background, the John Hancock Center, and to the right, the waters of the Great Lakes. Knitting it all together is Lake Shore Drive heading north.

120-121 Chicago breathes the fresh air of its "sea" on this hazy morning. The life of a metropolis that has a daily appointment with the future runs on the tracks of its elevated train in the shade of the buildings along the Magnificent Mile.

122 and 123 The Navy Pier was built at the mouth of the Chicago River in 1916 to facilitate the activities of merchant shipping. However, by the 1940s this place had been entirely dedicated to commerce and entertainment, where people could take a stroll against the backdrop of the city landscape. After the 190 million dollar rebuilding project of 1991, it is now an entertainment area with a 148 feet high wheel based on the original design of the one built in 1893.

124-125 Lake Michigan, the Navy Pier, and the unmistakable skyline of the city that made use of the lake to provide the baptismal water for the most daring architectural construction of the modern world: the skyscraper.

126-127 The flags that flap and crack in the wind on the Navy Pier platform are a perfect reminder of the changing character of the Windy City. For enthusiasts of sailing sports, they are irresistible.

128 The cruisers that leave from the Navy Pier offer an unusual and interesting trip along the lake shore and up the Chicago River, taking in some of the city's most famous sights, for example, the Sears Tower, the Buckingham Fountain, the Shedd Aquarium, and the downtown cityscape.

129 Much has been done so that the Navy Pier can offer entertainment for the whole family, from the Chicago Childrens Museum (top) to the big ferris wheel (bottom).

THE LAKEFRONT

132-133 Crowded beaches and ports in Lincoln Park: the shores of Lake Michigan are home to thirty or so beaches which are some of America's most popular during the summer months.

134-135 Oak Street Beach, the "St. Tropez of the Midwest," lies below the skyscrapers at the start of Lincoln Park and the Gold Coast.

130 and 131 By night Chicago seems different, in some ways warmer and more engaging. The streams of light and color that follow the edge of the lake along Lake Shore

Drive blur into a single golden flow as they pass the Navy Pier, a glowing spectacle of sound and light that revolves around the glittering ferris wheel.

136 and 137 The Lakefront is fun whether on foot or by bicycle. On one side there is the lake, which carries the scents of the Great North, on the other, the designs of the most famous architects in the world. In between, extends a long strip of parks, gardens, and beaches.

138 and 139 As
one heads north, the
skyscrapers thin out
and the number of
green areas and
bays reserved for
sailing increase.
Chicago gives the
impression of a city
with a very high
quality of life.
Lying between the
Great Plains and
the waters of an
inland sea, Chicago
proudly displays
itself to the world in
a magnificent
skyline as bold as

the Tower of Babel.
Chicago is at pace
with time, preceeds
it then stops, takes
a look back, and
gazes in the mirror
of its steel symbols,
of the Great Plains
sky, and of the
waves of an
immense inner sea.

140-141 A bay and
a port: this could be
a view from the
Mediterranean Côte
d'Azur transplanted
to the American
Midwest.

142 and 143
These are
artificially created
ports alongside
Lincoln Park. Lake
Michigan covers
22,394 square
miles and is the

only one of the
Great Lakes that
lies entirely within
the borders of the
United States. The
basin it fills was
created more than
10,000 years ago

and reaches a depth
of 919 feet. It
provides
opportunities for a
wide variety of
water sports, of
which sailing is the
most popular.

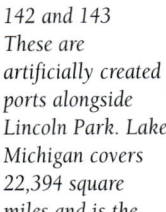

144 and 145 Lake Michigan is the other extraordinary landmark of Chicago. It is a panorama that has not emerged from the T-square and compasses of man but is the result of a different process. It is also Chicago's "sea," sun, wind, and waves.

146-147 Lake Michigan is great for sailing, cruising, fishing, or simply relaxing on the water. Just keep an eye on the current, the weather, the dangers derived from sailing close to the coast, and the temperature of the water.

148-149 The waves, the beach, the raucous cries of the seagulls: they are part of seemingly Caribbean scenes in the heart of the United States. This is a reality that is not to be found in the stockmarket listings, in the lists of the specialized magazines, or in the business and financial papers. It is a reality that lives and breathes, with the waves, the beach, and the seagulls.

148 bottom and 149 Chicago's lakeside offers an almost infinite choice of sports and relaxation activities. Skaters, joggers, and cyclists are common sights. The group shown on a beach to the north of the city appears to belong to a sports club, one of the many amateur associations based in Chicago.

150-151 Lake Michigan, a boat, and adventure: for the inhabitants of Chicago, daily life is not just business, the stock exchange, and skyscrapers. Set in gardens, silent and surprising monuments reflect the city's cosmopolitan spirit. This is the Baha'i House of Worship in Wilmette.

152-153 The evening shadows stretch out on the Calvary Cemetery in Evanston, on the northern metropolitan side of Chicago. A few miles away stands the Graceland Cemetery, another historical and more evocative place in Chicago.

154 and 155
Chicago is also famous for its public lawns, its parks, and sports (both supported or played). It has teams in all the professional major leagues most popular with the American public: in basketball, the Bulls, the former team of Michael Jordan, the world's most famous player, in American football, the Bears, in hockey, the Blackhawks, and in baseball, the White Sox and the Cubs.

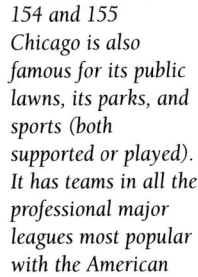

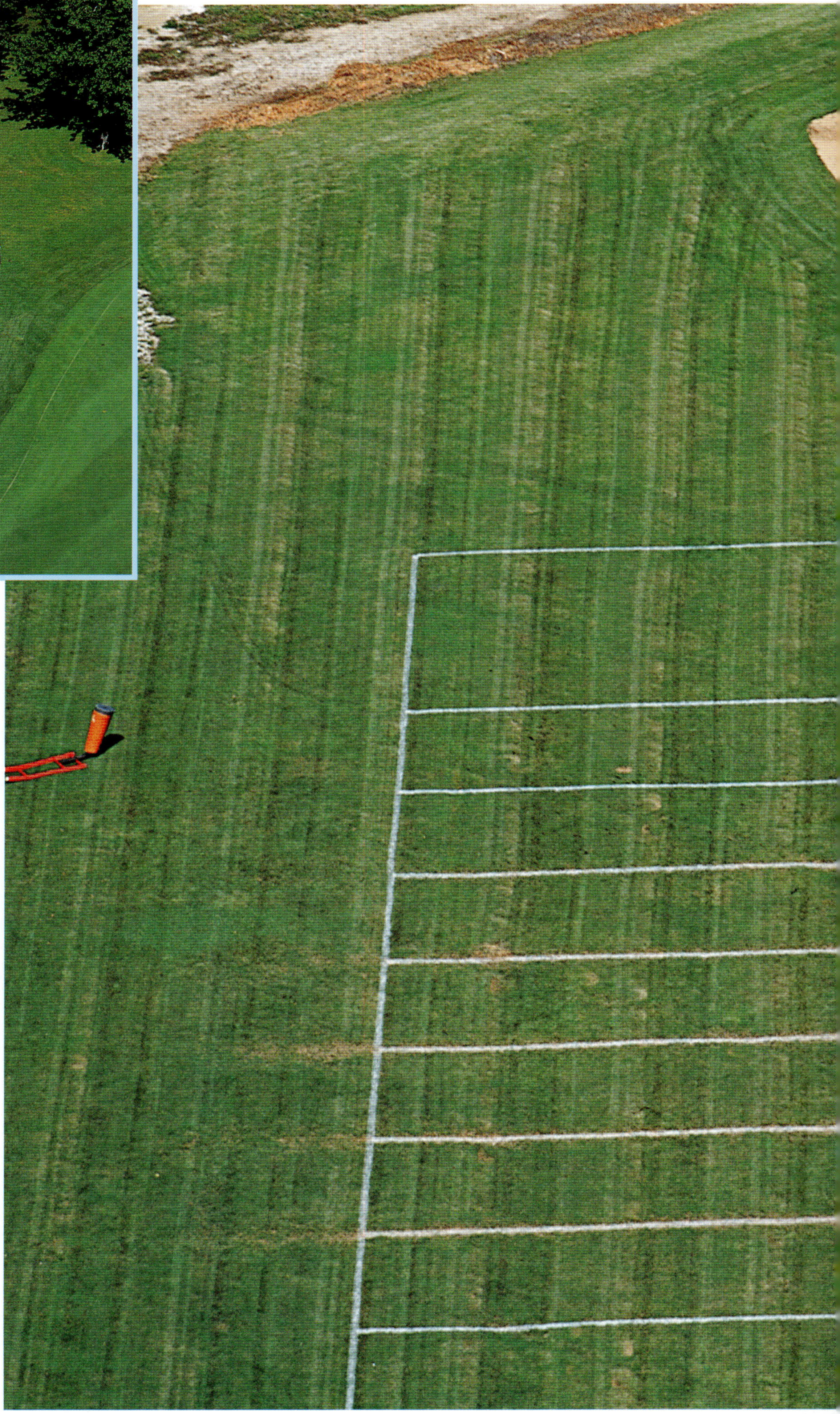

156-157 The North Side of Chicago has the very best that an American city can offer from an environmental viewpoint. The center of attraction in the vast, low density area is Lincoln Park, which covers 1,211 acres stretched along 6.5 miles of the Lake Michigan shoreline. It offers a variety of attractions such as historical buildings, temples, museums, and greenhouses like the Lincoln Park Conservatory (bottom photograph).

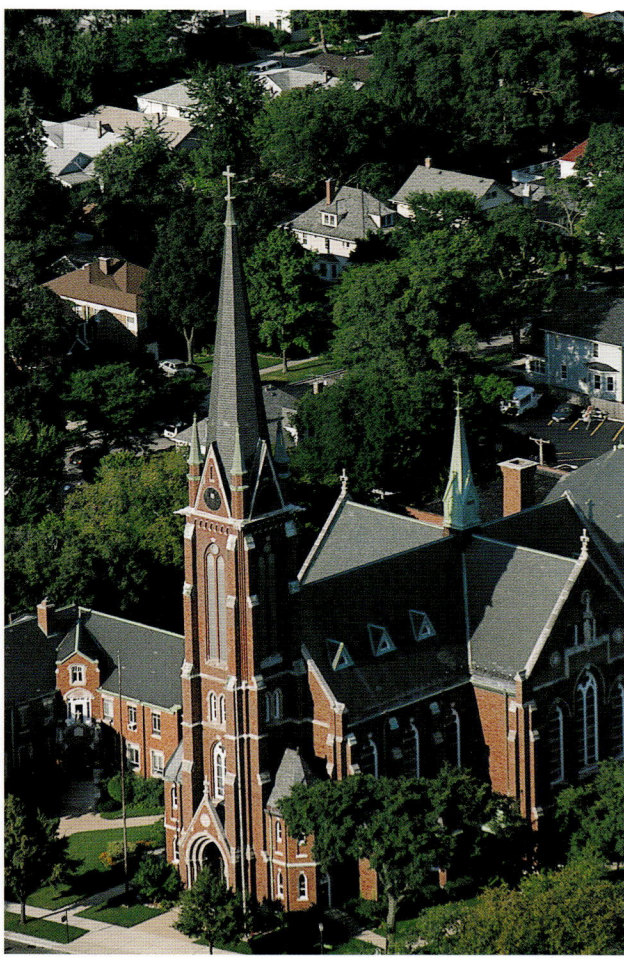

158-159 Every shade of blue, the beach, and large sand dunes all immersed in a sea of green: this is Lake Michigan on the South Side where Illinois borders Indiana. Beaches like this one draw summer visitors from both Chicago and Detroit.

160 *Vertical and horizontal, concentrated and sprawling, unified and divided, Chicago represents a long list of adjectives and their opposites. It stands at* *the gates to the Great Plains, is unique, full of vitality, often contradictory, and always fascinating. In the Big Onion, open spaces and urban labyrinths are* *merged in avant-garde architectural projects. The Chicago River is a path that leads to Lake Michigan, the Great Lakes, and the call of the North.*

PHOTO CREDITS

All the pictures inside the book are by Antonio Attini except for the following:

Marcello Bertinetti/Archivio White Star: pages 37, 38, 40.

Chicago Historical Society: pages 24-25, 26 left, 27 bottom right, 28.

Chicago Public Library: pages 30 top, 31 top.

Corbis/Grazia Neri: pages 34, 35 top, 36 bottom left.

Library of Congress, Washington, D.C.: pages 26-27 top, 30-31 bottom, 32-33.

NASA Archives: pages. 16 top, 16 bottom, 16-17.

TopFoto/ICP: page 35 bottom.